A bearded AMISH gentlemen drives his buggy past one of the many one-room schoolhouses in the AMISH COUNTRY. The visitor is encouraged to leave the highway and take to the "backroads" in the area, for it is here that he will come upon scenes such as this.

The AMISH COUNTRY is, perhaps, one of the most picturesque areas in Pennsylvania. Local residents both AMISH and NON-AMISH are proud of their homes and business places, they are well kept and noted for their cleanliness. An AMISH Carriage passing a planting of brightly colored flowers adds to the beauty.

The Amish Home.....

The home is the center of AMISH life; Church services are held in the home, most entertainment is in the home, babies are born here, weddings and funerals are held in the home.

Some noticable features of an AMISH home are the absence of electric wires, a large porch and usually a neat fence around the yard.

Many AMISH homes are really three homes in one, sections are built onto the original house for grandparents and still another section for a son and his wife making a three generation house as pictured below.

An AMISH kitchen is a functional room, all meals are served in the kitchen, brightly colored appointments may be found; but only if they serve a purpose.

Lighting is always by kerosene or gasoline lamps, never by electricity. The wood or coal burning range is used for cooking and heating.

Not only does the kitchen serve as a dining room, it is also the family recreation room. The kitchen is ususally the largest room in the house.

There is no plumbing, water is carried into the house for cooking, drinking and bathing.

Photo Courtesy, Amish Village Inc.

Photo Courtesy, Amish Farm and House

The living or "front" room is used only on special occasions such as weddings, church or visits from very important persons, normal entertaining of guests is done in the kitchen. The benches serve as pews for church services.

Windowshades or blinds are kept drawn to insure privacy, since the AMISH do not use curtains or draperies.

An AMISH bedroom is like the rest of the house, practical with no pictures or other forms of wall decorations with the exception of an occasional Bible Verse or useful calendar.

Handmade quilts adorn the beds, brightly colored with intricate designs, they are made to last a lifetime.

Photo Courtesy, Plain & Fancy Farm

Water Wheels.....

The water wheel is a major source of power for the AMISH farm. Located in a nearby stream, the wheel will operate a pump in the house or barn by means of a wire or cable stretching as far as a half mile.

There are several different types of water wheels along the streams in the AMISH COUNTRY.

Many water wheels are surrounded by concrete walls or wire fences; to keep cattle grazing in the meadow from injury should they step into the wheel.

Photo by Jim Hess Amish Homestead

Wind Wheel.....

Another major source of power on the AMISH farm is the Wind Wheel or Windmill. The wheel pictured, said to be the largest in the area is located east of Intercourse, Pa., along route 340.

The rudder-like tail behind the wheel keeps the spinning blades pointing into the wind harnessing the natural power.

This wheel operates two pumps drawing water from separate wells feeding into the large standing tank. The water flows by gravity from the tank, through pipes, to several farms and homes in the immediate vicinity.

Bridges.....

Covered bridges are scattered throughout the AMISH COUNTRY. They are fast being replaced by counterparts of steel and concrete; some are being saved. Built of wood the bridges have stood up to modern modes of transportation and fear only two enemies, floods and fire.

Have patience when you come upon one of the bridges and it won't be long until you hear the clip-clop of a horse drawn buggy crossing the bridge. If the sound should stop midway through the bridge, you will know the occupants are enjoying the tradition which has earned the name "Kissing Bridge".

We have noted that often an automobile will pause as it traverses the stream.

Amish at Work.....

Living by "The Book" with no modern machinery, the AMISH use horses and mules to power his farm equipment and to take his produce to market.

Farming is a year-round job and one may see different kinds of work being done in the various seasons of the year. The Wheat Harvest is in July, Tobacco in August, Corn in October, planting is done in April and May.

The farmer (above) is raking his crop of Hay, (left) Tobacco cutting and (below) AMISH farmers stack baled Corn Fodder.

Photo Courtesy, Jim Garrahy's Fudge Kitchen

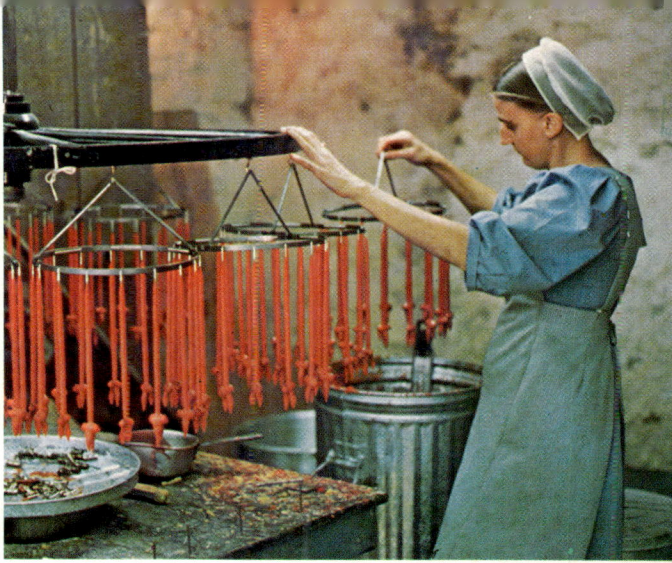

Photo Courtesy, Old Candle Barn

Some AMISH folk work at other than farming such as the two girls pictured, (left) making candy in a local fudge shop and (above) hand-dipping candles. AMISH may also be found cooking and serving in many of the restaurants located throughout the AMISH COUNTRY.

Men accept employment in several trades, the most popular being carpentry, some operate business places such as cabinet-makers; Carriage-shops, and other not-too-worldly positions.

The AMISH woman (below) is working in one of the many bake-shops in the AMISH COUNTRY. She is shown removing a "batch" of Shoo-Fly Pies, tasty and gocey from the oven.

Photo Courtesy of Dutch Haven

Amish Farming.....

AMISH farmers work from sun-up to sun-down. Their varied chores present an endless array of picture possibilities.

Farming is a family operation and the AMISH family is large, by today's standards, the children and the women take an active part in working the fields from planting to harvest.

Crops include corn, hay, small grains, tobacco, potatoes, beans, tomatos and fruit in addition to beef, pork and poultry. Much of the acreage is used to raise feed for the livestock.

An AMISH boy driving a wagon load of wheat sheaves from the field where the ripe wheat was cut by a horse-drawn reaper. The load will be hauled to the barn where it will be threshed to separate the grain from the straw.

A farm without cows would be like a city without taxi cabs. Dairy farming is popular among the AMISH. This herd of holstein cows is grazing in the meadow while the farmer prepares a field for planting.

The AMISH farms are not large, eighty to one hundred twenty acres being an average farmstead. Their neighbors are close and when help is needed they may be depended upon to supply the manpower in order to get the work finished.

Scenes like those pictured on these pages are commonplace in the AMISH COUNTRY, however, it is necessary to leave the highways and traverse the side roads to find the solitude needed to fully appreciate this unique culture.

The AMISH in the fields are testimonials to their belief in non-conformity and love for the rural life.

It is not unusual to find AMISH women handling a team of horses or mules doing men's work in the fields.

Wheat Harvest in the Amish Country.....

Bonnets.....

AMISH women always wear a head covering known as a prayer cap. The tradition is based on the Bible (1 Cor. 11:5) which states, "Every woman that prayeth or prophesieth with her head uncovered dishonoureth her head." The prayer cap is always white, made of organdy and tied with a bow.

Dresses are cut from the same pattern, there is no style competition among the women. Solid colors are permitted, usually black, maroon, green, blue or tan.

An apron is often worn over the dress, married women wear black or colored aprons, unmarried girls wear white aprons.

AMISH women do not cut their hair for it is written, "It is a shame for a woman to be shorn or shaven", (1 Cor. 11:6).

Photo by Robert Haycock, Pa. State Police Fire Marshal

Barn Raising.....

One of the AMISH COUNTRY'S oldest traditions is the Barn Raising. Should fire strike an AMISH barn, his friends and neighbors gather usually within two weeks and at sunrise the work begins. By noon the sides and ends are "raised" and swarms of men scamper over the frame work nailing on the roof and siding.

The work is hard; but there is much fun and fellowship along with competitive spirit making the day move fast. By nightfall the barn is virtually finished and another cooperative effort has been completed.

The women and children are not left out, serving lunch to more than 200 workers is a monumental task and all hands are needed to prepare the feast.

Aerial View of Amish Country

Barefeet.....

AMISH children are very colorful with their miniature clothing made just like the grown-ups. The boys wear straw-hats and the girls wear bonnets over their white prayer caps.

AMISH youngsters have a just scrubbed look and usually display bright smiles reflecting the happy lives they enjoy.

They attend one-room schools, have no bus service and are through with education after the eighth grade.

Photo by Robert P. Frey

Photo by Robert P. Frey

There are two kinds of buggies seen in the AMISH COUNTRY, the Box-like Family Carriage (left) and the open Courting Buggy (above).

There are also several other wagons and carts which travel the roads in the area, always pulled by well groomed horses.

A very rare picture is this young family riding in a Courting Buggy. Traditionally a married couple will use a Family Carriage not a Courting Buggy (the difference being Courting Buggies are not covered and Family Carriages have a seat in the rear for the children).

An AMISH elder explained this picture, "While it makes good sense to protect your family from the wind and rain, there is no church rule which forbids a married man from taking his wife and kiddies out for a ride in an open buggy, if the weather is good and the buggy is handy."

The picture was made in 1957 near White Horse along route 340 east of Intercourse, Pa. by Marshall Dussinger.

The AMISH drive their horses and buggies, not because they feel the automobile is wicked; but because they believe the kind of living brought on by the automobile would break down the family unit and the structure of their community.

The AMISH are very proud of their horses and the children learn at a very young age how to care for the animals. The horse is an important part of AMISH life, and the responsibility of their grooming and feeding is a part of the children's education.

AMISH buggies are built by local craftsmen and repairs, when needed, are usually done by the owners.
State law has forced the AMISH to equip the buggies with battery operated lights for safety.

Church rules do not prohibit the AMISH from riding in automobiles, other forms of transportation used include busses and trains.

Pictured on these pages are the two kinds of buggies in many locations and at different times of the year. There is no special season to see the buggies, they are always there in the AMISH COUNTRY.

Bird-In-Hand....

The village of Bird-In-Hand is located along route 340 east of Lancaster, Pa. Known as the Old Philadelphia Pike, this road was once the King's Highway (the oldest road in the United States) leading from Philadelphia to Lancaster, the oldest inland city in the country.

Above, a unique double team hitch pulling an AMISH Family Carriage; left, a group of children in their Sunday Dress; below, parking outside the Old Village Store.

Beards.....

AMISH beards come in a variety of size, shape and color; but one thing is common, they are worn only by married men and never with a moustache.

The man's clothing is always black, trousers are held up by suspenders, no belts; shirts may be any plain color, and neckties (since they have no practical purpose) are not worn. Most AMISH suits are made by the women-folk at home, very few are "store-bought".

AMISH believe that the Scriptures teach separation between church and world, they feel it is not possible for a church to keep its values if members associate with people who hold different beliefs, or none at all.

They keep the same dress as they have for centuries, for they see no need to be changing styles with the changing times.

Wide brimmed hats, either black felt or straw depending on the weather are worn by both the men and boys.

Photo by Bill Gallagher

Amish Farms . . . . .

The AMISH farmstead is usually located at the end of a long lane. In addition to the farmhouse, and very large barn, there are often several out-buildings—corn bin, chicken house, tobacco barn, milk house and a tall silo.

White is the predominent color although some AMISH barns are painted yellow or red. They never use Hex Signs or lightning rods.

Faith, Family, Friendship and Farming are the basic principles of AMISH life, and it all takes place on the Farm.

Intercourse, Pennsylvania . . . . .

The village of Intercourse is located east of Lancaster, Pa., along Route 340. Surrounded by AMISH farms, Intercourse is considered to be the center of the AMISH COUNTRY.

The village contains many shops and stores which are patronized by the AMISH. An outstanding feature of the business places in Intercourse is the hitching posts in front, for many of the customers travel by horse and buggy and need this facility.

Below, an AMISH carriage towing a second carriage.

No visit to the AMISH COUNTRY is complete without spending some time in "downtown" Intercourse; but don't be in a hurry. Park your car and walk, the distance is not too far and a leisurely stroll around the town will be rewarding.

Intercourse may well be the only place in the country where Horse and Buggy traffic, sometimes, outnumbers that of Automobiles. A few hours spent on the sidewalks will offer you a close-up view of AMISH life and you will see many different kinds of horse-drawn vehicles traveling the streets.

Intercourse, Pennsylvania.....

The name of the village is said to be derived from the intersection or "intercourse" of two major highways.

The King's Highway (route 340) runs east and west and was once a major route from Philadelphia to Harrisburg. Newport Road (route 772) enters from the south and was an important connection with the sea through the Pequea Valley to Newport, Delaware.

Intercourse is, today a center for visitors to the Pennsylvania Dutch Country.

Barns.....

The Bank Barn, an outstanding feature of the AMISH Barn is the two story building with a bank of ground piled up to the second story level enabling loaded wagons to be pulled into the barn on both levels.

Below is a loaded tobacco wagon and team of mules waiting in front of the tobacco barn. The tobacco will be hung in the barn until it is air-cured and ready for stripping.

An AMISH girl, (above) taking down the wash on a Monday afternoon. Doing household chores is an important part of the AMISH education, and children begin at an early age to help their Mothers.

At right, an AMISH-MAN is delayed at a grade crossing while the STRASBURG RAILROAD steams past on the "Road to Paradise", with a load of tourists.

Photo Courtesy Strasburg Railroad

Markets.....

Farmer's Markets are found throughout the AMISH COUNTRY. The AMISH girl (above) is "Tending Market" where produce from the farm is offered to the public at reasonable prices.

Very young children (right) may be found selling at the markets. While there are many markets and roadside produce stands in the area the hours and days do vary unlike the normal business days of our modern supermarkets.

Below, another form of produce marketing is the selling of grain or buying feed from the local mills. From a wagon pulled by horses, the grain is hoisted to the upper floor of the mill by rope pulley.

Photo Courtesy, Mill Bridge Craft Village

Photo Courtesy, Weavertown One Room School

Route 340 . . . . .

Pennsylvania Route 340, the Heart of the AMISH COUNTRY in the Land of the Pennsylvania Dutch.

The Old Philadelphia Pike was once the King's Highway (the oldest road in the United States) leading from Philadelphia to Lancaster, Pa., the oldest inland city in the country, laid out in 1730.

Today the road is much the same, in fact no other highway carries as much horse-and-buggy traffic than does Route 340 between Lancaster and Intercourse.

The photograph at left shows the AMISH Family Carriage with the seat in the back for the children, often they look out the rear window as the carriage travels down the road.

Below are two scenes along Route 340, many of the pictures in this book were made on this road; but do not think that Route 340 is the only road in the AMISH COUNTRY, there are many more all reaching out to the East and Southeast of Lancaster.

Winter in the Amish Country . . . . .

May we suggest the AMISH COUNTRY during the winter months? Granted most visitors spend time here only during the summer, and surely the growing season is more colorful.

The AMISH are a hardy people, they do not spend the cold days indoors. Winter will offer a different view, many of the buggies are replaced with horse-drawn sleighs complete with bells (right), straw hats are replaced with broad-brimmed black felt and barefeet are covered with shoes.

The children still walk to school, afterwards, when farm and household chores are finished they find time to play as the group below.